The Eyes of Heaven

The Eyes of Heaven

Beverley Cooper

The Eyes of Heaven
first published 2010 by
Scirocco Drama
An imprint of J. Gordon Shillingford Publishing Inc.
© 2010 Beverley Cooper

Scirocco Drama Editor: Glenda MacFarlane
Cover design by Terry Gallagher/Doowah Design Inc.
Author photo by Corrine Koslo
Printed and bound in Canada on 100% post-consumer recycled paper.

We acknowledge the financial support of the Manitoba Arts Council, The Canada
Council for the Arts and the Government of Canada through the Book Publishing
Industry Development Program (BPIDP) for our publishing program.

Library and Archives Canada Cataloguing in Publication

Cooper, Beverley
    The eyes of heaven / Beverley Cooper.

A play.
ISBN 978-1-897289-48-8

I. Title.

PS8555.O5884E94 2010   C812'.54   C2010-901723-4

J. Gordon Shillingford Publishing
P.O. Box 86, RPO Corydon Avenue, Winnipeg, MB Canada R3M 3S3

In memory of my father—
who taught me so much about laughter, love and courage.

Beverley Cooper

Beverley has written for theatre, TV and film. Beverley's writing for theatre includes *Thin Ice* (co-written with Banuta Rubess) which won Dora and Chalmer's Awards, published by Playwrights Canada Press, *Clue in the Fast Lane* (co-written with Ann-Marie MacDonald) and *The Woman in White* (adapted from the novel by Wilkie Collins) which was produced at Theatre Aquarius in 2008. Her play *Innocence Lost: A Play about Steven Truscott* was a sold-out hit at the Blyth Festival in both 2008 and 2009 and was nominated for a Governor General's Literary Award. *Innocence Lost* is published by Scirocco Drama, 2009. Beverley was invited to speak and read from *Innocence Lost* at the 2009 Women Playwrights International conference in Mumbai, India. She has written extensively for CBC radio drama; both original dramas and adaptations. Her adaptation of Rohinton Mistry's epic novel *A Fine Balance* and her original drama *It Came from Beyond!* both earned her nominations for a Writer's Guild of Canada Award. She worked as the story editor on the award winning radio series *Afghanada*, as well as producing the second season and directing five episodes. She has dramatized the following books for radio: *Alias Grace, Away, The Secret World of Og* (Silver Medal Award Winner, New York Festival, International Radio Awards) and *The Englishman's Boy*. Other original dramas include the hugely popular series *The Super Adventures of Mary Marvelous* and several episodes of *Hartfeldt, Saskatchewan*. Beverley's television writing credits include episodes of *Ready or Not, Sesame Park* and *Street Legal*. She has also written a film script entitled *The Partly True Story of Pearl Heart*. Beverley trained as an actor at Studio 58 in Vancouver, and has performed in TV, film and in theatres across the country. Beverley is a member of PEN Canada: an organization that assists writers around the world who are persecuted for the peaceful expression of their ideas. She lives in Toronto, Canada with her actor husband, John Jarvis and two wonderful sons, Will and Mac.

Cast

Glenn Bernhardt: mid/late forties, mum

Eloise Bernhardt: 15, her daughter

Christine Clark: 24, university student

Nic Barlow: 30ish, African-Canadian

Setting

A farmhouse in the country, mid September, surrounded by cornfields. A kitchen with a screen door that leads to an outdoor porch. Both the kitchen and the porch are playing areas. There is a staircase in the kitchen leading upstairs.

Production Credits

The Eyes of Heaven premiered at the Blyth Festival, under the Artistic Directorship of Eric Coates, on June 26, 2007, with the following cast.

GLENN Bernhardt – Susan Stackhouse

ELOISE Bernhardt – Laura Schutt

CHRISTINE Clark - Andrea Donaldson

NIC Barlow – Andrew Moodie

Directed by Gina Wilkinson

Set and Costume Design by Pat Flood

Lighting Design by Louise Guinand

Sound Design by Todd Charlton

Stage Manager: Shauna Japp

Assistant Stage Manager: Joanna Barrotta

Assistant Director: Andrea Donaldson

Playwright's Notes

Where do ideas come from? That is a question that has been asked and answered by poets, philosophers and scientists for thousands of years. New ideas, new concepts, are sometimes thought provoking, sometimes dangerous, dangerous, and can challenge our very foundations. The idea for this play came from many sources; my personal love for the farmland in Huron County; memories of teenage angst; watching my father die from cancer with dignity and courage; and from gazing at the night sky, full of wonder. This is a story that questions what we believe in, examines how we judge each other and asks the universal question; "What is out there, beyond the stars?"

Many heartfelt thanks to Gina Wilkinson and Eric Coates for their amazing support, inspired ideas, generous spirits and vigorous dramaturgy. I would like to thank the original cast, Susan, Laura, Andrea and Andrew, for their enormous talent and commitment. Thanks also goes to; Capucine Onn for her insight; to the actors who participated in workshops and shared their thoughts, Marie Beath Badian, Raoul Bhaneja, Conrad Coates, Andrea Donaldson, Laurel Paetz, Laura Schutt and Tova Smith; Pat Flood and the Blyth Crew for the real corn that rustled in the breeze.

The Eyes of Heaven was developed with support from the Ontario Arts Council, Toronto Arts Council and Roulston Roy New Play Development Fund (Blyth Festival).

Act One

Scene 1

Early morning. GLENN is talking on a cordless phone while she putters around the kitchen, making breakfast; pouring orange juice, cutting up fruit, sipping coffee—all while...

GLENN: I feel like there's a firestorm waiting inside of me, and it's going to be sparked up anytime. One minute I'm going along fine, and then blood rushes to my head, my hands, my feet, I'm dripping sweat and I want to throttle everyone I meet. My moods are up and down like a bobbing poodle dog. Yesterday Ellie found me with my head in the freezer. She keeps telling me to get out more but nobody wants to be around a menopausal woman or peri-menopausal or what ever they call it—nobody wants to see our hormones paraded in public... Ohhh, just you wait, it's just one more thing they don't tell you about female plumbing. Remember those classes when they put all us girls in one room and showed a movie; "Growing Up and Liking it"? They should have shown us the sequel: "Aging Badly and Not Liking It One Bit"... And my memory is all out of whack too. I'm losing my nouns. I reach for them and they are not there, I stare at that... "thing, that thing" for a full minute while I root around in the old memory cabinet for the word "toaster"... *(Covers phone and calls upstairs.)* Breakfast! *(Back to phone.)* So anyway... Friday night... *(Lowers her voice.)* ...she's bucking to go to some party with that gang of hoodlums

I was telling you about... They all wear hoods up over their heads and grunt... I have no intention of letting her go. Over my dead body. She's got to get her marks back up before I even think about... Yes, they're way down. *(Regular voice.)* Have you got any glads left standing? Mine got hit by that blast of hail... Oh... Just a sec.

ELOISE comes down the stairs, still half asleep and in pyjama bottoms and a T-shirt, her hair dishevelled.

GLENN: Good-morning, Sleeping Beauty. What kind of cereal?

ELOISE: I can get my own.

GLENN: Suit yourself.

ELOISE picks up the orange juice her mother has poured, pours it down the sink, then proceeds to make herself chocolate milk, with lots of chocolate and a piece of toast with sugar and cinnamon as...

(Back to phone—low.) Alright, I've got to go in a minute but have you talked to Theresa?... I guess she's not talking to anyone. Poor thing. I wouldn't either. I'd want to kill him. If she wants to do away with her husband just get her to lock him in with me while I'm having a hot flash and I'll take care of all her problems... Well I *know*! If I was a parent with a kid in that woman's classroom I wouldn't be sending my husband into any parent/teacher meetings on his own—

ELOISE: You don't have a husband.

GLENN: And then poor Theresa has to look at "her" every day. With her child in the same classroom. I can't believe the board didn't turf her. Course they can't do a thing with that union staring them down. Out of this world when a teacher can...have a you know what—

ELOISE: I already know all about it. Miss Lewis is having hot sex with a parent of one of her students.

GLENN: Eloise.

ELOISE: What do you want me to call it…"having an affair"? That saying is so bizarre. Like it's a lawn party or something.

GLENN: Love shmuv. All I know is if it was me, I'd run her out of town. Tar and feather my husband and—

ELOISE: I keep telling you, you don't have a husband.

GLENN: Though from what I understand Theresa's no picnic either—did you see what she wore to the Sunday night supper? One more feather on that hat and someone would have squawked at her. Talk about overdressed for an occasion…I'd better go. I've got to make sure Ellie gets out the door…I'll ask her and let you know…alright then… I will… Yeah, I have to go root and forage at the Value-Mart for something for dinner and Ellie needs new underwear and well I've got a list as long as…Ron Hooper's hair. Have you seen him lately? Right down his back… Anyhoo, I'll call you when I can.

GLENN hangs up the phone.

ELOISE: Ask her what?

GLENN: Aunty Bobbie wants to take you out for your birthday.

ELOISE: Why did you all get boys' names?

GLENN: Don't start.

ELOISE: It's so weird. Glenn, Bobbie, Jamie. Three girls all with boys' names.

GLENN: It's too early in the morning for this conversation because I already know where it is going.

ELOISE: I have a new theory.

GLENN: Yeah?

ELOISE: Grandad was hoping you'd all leave the toilet seat up for him.

GLENN: Can we please stick to the topic?

ELOISE: Out where?

GLENN: Someplace nice. For dinner. On the Saturday after.

ELOISE: Where nice?

GLENN: She was thinking the Candlelight but if you want to suggest—

ELOISE: She thinks the Candlelight is nice? Last time we went they tried to give me crayons and a colour page.

GLENN: —if you want to suggest some place else I am sure she would be happy to— How about Stratford? There's a couple of new spots there. Maybe you could go to a play after.

ELOISE: Some Shakespeare shit?

GLENN: Ellie. Aunty Bobbie just wants to take you somewhere you'd like.

ELOISE: I don't want to see any boring Shakespeare. When I went with school I was sitting near the front and some dimbo kept twanging Smarties at the stage and hitting the back of my head. I couldn't understand a word they were saying, "Methinks this and M'lord that." It's shit.

GLENN: Alright! Stop using that word!

ELOISE: It's part of life, Mum, comes out of your bum.

GLENN: *You* call Aunty Bobbie and work it out with her.

Perhaps you will deign to speak civilly to her. It seems I don't rate for respect.

ELOISE: Give me a break.

GLENN: No. You give me a break.

> *Long silence. ELOISE pours more sugar on her toast. GLENN makes ELOISE's lunch.*

You used to like the plays at Stratford.

ELOISE: When?

GLENN: When Daddy took you to see *Romeo and Juliet,* for weeks afterwards you would pretend you were Juliet and he was your Romeo.

ELOISE: Don't you dare go down memory lane. Don't you dare.

GLENN: Fine. I just don't want you revising history. That's all.

> *Pause.*

Did you get your homework all done?

ELOISE: Most of it.

GLENN: What does that mean?

ELOISE: I don't understand the science stuff.

GLENN: Ellie. Science used to be your best subject.

> *Pause.*

Is there time before school to talk to your teacher?

ELOISE: I can't understand him.

GLENN: Who?

ELOISE: My science teacher. I don't know what he's talking about.

GLENN: He's the new one right? The dark man?

ELOISE: Give me a break, Mother. He's Black.

GLENN: Well I can't keep up with the proper terms for every race in this world. What's the problem, does he have some sort of accent?

ELOISE: No. He's just a goof. He talks like he thinks science is some big fun secret that he's going to let us in on. He gets all excited and starts waving his hands around. He keeps saying "Think for yourself! Don't believe something just because it's in a textbook." Meanwhile we have a test the next day and the only thing we've got to go on is the textbook. He's a total goof.

GLENN: Maybe he's just trying to make it interesting for you.

ELOISE: Yeah, right.

GLENN: Is he any relation to those people working at the rutabaga factory?

ELOISE: No. Not all Black people are related, Mum.

GLENN: I was just asking. It was a perfectly harmless question.

ELOISE: Those guys who work in the rutabaga factory are from Jamaica. He's from Toronto.

GLENN: Alright. Alright. Can Liz help you with Science?

ELOISE: Liz? Ha. She doesn't even listen. She's too busy fantasizing. She thinks he's "gorgeous." She rushes up after class and asks stupid questions. *(Batting her eyelashes.)* " I don't understand the unit on plant vegetation"—flutter—flutter.

GLENN: Well… She better not let her father know that.

ELOISE: Why?

GLENN: Well. Jim isn't known for being the most open minded kind of person.

ELOISE: It's not like she's going to marry him or anything. He's old. He's a teacher. She just likes him 'cause she wants to be different.

GLENN: I just hope she's careful. You hear all the time about teachers taking advantage of young people.

ELOISE: I think he's got more to worry about from Liz.

GLENN: What do you mean by that? Ellie, you aren't saying that Liz and he have—

ELOISE: No! It was a joke!

GLENN: Why has he come here anyway?

ELOISE: I don't know! I haven't asked him.

GLENN: I mean there are a lot more Black people in Toronto, he'd feel more at home there.

ELOISE: Oh, Mother.

GLENN: Don't you "Oh, Mother" me.

ELOISE: I'm just trying to wrap my brain around his weird concepts.

GLENN: Oh he's the one. I remember now. He has some radical ideas that got some folks hopping. He went to some meeting and acted know-it-all. Jane Barber said she was so mad after she just about ran over some poor Mennonites. Mind you Jane is a terrible driver at the best of times.

ELOISE: Mrs. Barber? She picks my ass.

GLENN: Well, my dear, he's your teacher for now. So you had better try to understand what he's talking about. I'll drive you in, so you can get there early.

ELOISE:　　I don't want to get there early.

> *GLENN cleans up a little. She puts the plate of fruit a little closer to ELOISE. ELOISE takes a piece and picks small bits of it off to eat, slowly before…*

Did you decide about the party yet?

> *GLENN sighs.*

GLENN:　　I just don't think it's a good idea.

ELOISE:　　Why?!

GLENN:　　Because I don't know these kids. I don't know their parents.

ELOISE:　　They're nice!

GLENN:　　That's not what I heard.

ELOISE:　　What have you heard?

GLENN:　　You were the one who said they were losers. That all the girls were going to end up in dead-end beauty salons doing cheap pedicures.

ELOISE:　　Mother! I said that two years ago. I didn't even know them. I thought they were weird at first. They look a little wild but they're not. They're all really normal.

GLENN:　　That's normal? Tattoos of snakes and rats are normal?

ELOISE:　　That's just one guy. And he's nice. He goes and reads to his granny, after school, three times a week.

GLENN:　　Who's going?

ELOISE:　　Everyone is going.

GLENN:　　Who's everyone?

ELOISE:	Janice. Connie… Liz.
GLENN:	Liz is going?
ELOISE:	Yes.
GLENN:	And Jim and Caroline are OK with that?
ELOISE:	I guess so.
GLENN:	That's hard to believe. They don't mind Liz being friends with these kids?
ELOISE:	It's a party, Mum, we're just hanging out. Come on. Please. For once? I won't be late.
GLENN:	How late is not late?
ELOISE:	One?
GLENN:	Is there going to be drinking?
ELOISE:	I don't know! Maybe. But I don't drink. I never drink.
GLENN:	Eloise… I just—
ELOISE:	Don't baby me. I'm almost sixteen. You never let me do anything… You have to let go sometime.
GLENN:	What comic did you read that in? *True Romance*?
ELOISE:	You see? I don't even read comics any more.
GLENN:	I am not babying you. I am trying to make sure you are not getting into a bad situation with bad people.
ELOISE:	Why do you have to judge people all the time? You don't know anything about them. You think, just because they don't have a lot of money, or they dress differently that—
GLENN:	You don't know what I am thinking.

ELOISE: Yes I do. You think it would be easier for you if I don't go and then you don't have to worry.

GLENN: I'll worry if you go and I'll worry if you don't go. I worry if I buy you the right kind of socks or not.

ELOISE: Stop trying to control every friggin' little thing I do. I'm like some kind of freak with my mother following me around, watching my every move. I hate it!

GLENN: Ellie…please don't… Let's just talk this through.

ELOISE: No. You watch me like a bug in a cage.

GLENN: I do not.

ELOISE: This is a really hard year for me. I feel like everyone is changing all over the place…and I don't know where I fit in anymore…

GLENN: Oh sweetheart.

ELOISE: Liz is being really weird and she wants me to go and I'm afraid if I don't—

GLENN: How is Liz being weird? You've been friends for so long… Do you want me to talk to her?

ELOISE: No! I shouldn't have told you. I should never tell you anything.

Pause.

GLENN: Alright.

Pause.

But here's the deal. You have to be home by midnight. I don't want you wearing that short red leather thing or too much make-up.

ELOISE: I can go?

GLENN: Yes.

> *ELOISE makes a small delighted squeal.*

But, I'm going to drive you there and back—

ELOISE: I can get a ride with Liz's brother.

GLENN: Kevin? I thought he was at Waterloo.

ELOISE: I guess he's home for the weekend.

GLENN: Good, you can ask him about Waterloo. I hear that's a really good option.

ELOISE: Mum, I'm not talking to Kevin about universities.

GLENN: No drinking at all…do you hear me?

ELOISE: Yes!

GLENN: Just please don't say I never let you do anything.

ELOISE: OK.

GLENN: You can take my cell phone just in case.

ELOISE: OK.

> *Noticing time:*

GLENN: Oh dear Lord, the bus'll be here any minute. Run and get dressed! I've still got to throw your lunch together.

> *ELOISE runs upstairs to get dressed. GLENN hurries to put the lunch in the lunch bag with a cool pack and drink. Then she calls up the stairs.*

Comb the back of your hair, it looks like a small rodent has made a nest back there, and you've got smudge under your eyes.

ELOISE: *(O/S.)* I know!

GLENN: And hurry it up.

ELOISE: *(O/S.)* Stop yelling at me!

> *GLENN looks out the door towards the road. She looks up at the sky to check the weather and then back to the road. She speaks to an unseen person.*

GLENN: I know what you're thinking... But I'm trying, OK? I am really trying.

Scene 2

Late Friday night. It is very dark except for the outside porch light. The sound of crickets fill the air. Everything is still except for a slight rustling of the corn. After a moment, now dressed in her party clothes, ELOISE rushes out of the cornfield. She has been running and is out of breath. She gulps air for a moment then suddenly freezes. Something rustles in the corn behind her. But it is slight, probably just the wind. ELOISE is tense, wary. After a moment she releases her breath and takes stock of her clothes. Her dress has a rip. She rubs off her lipstick, fixes her hair... Then she slips off her shoes and tip-toes quietly up the stairs towards the back door. Out of the shadows comes a voice.

GLENN: Are you aware of what time it is?

The voice momentarily frightens ELOISE and she freezes, terrified.

Perhaps your watch stopped. Perhaps you mislaid my cell or couldn't remember our phone number. Maybe you were just having so much fun you lost track of time. I can't wait for what excuse you are going to come up with because I can tell it's really going to be juicy.

Pause.

I was just sitting here, remembering the day you told me the sky was green. You were four. I told you it was blue but you didn't go for it. You were sure it was green. At first I thought maybe you were mixing your colours up but that wasn't the case.

You knew the difference between green and blue. You just weren't going to see what I saw, you were going to look at things your own way and nothing was going to change that.

Pause.

Are you going to tell me now that that the sky is green? Is that what you are going to tell me? That I'm crazy and over protective and that I baby you because I want you home, safe, before two in the morning?

Pause.

You really pulled a fast one over me this time. I almost believed you.

ELOISE: Can I go inside now?

       GLENN emerges from the darkness but looks somewhat menacing in the half light.

GLENN: At about twelve-thirty I started to get worried. But no, I told myself, she's a big girl and she said she'd be home by midnight so she'll be here soon. After one o'clock I started to think maybe the phone lines were down. But they weren't because I was able to call my cell. Of course you didn't have it turned on. So I called Liz's house and spoke to Jim. He said *his daughter* had been home for ages—apparently Liz said she couldn't find you when she and Kevin wanted to leave, that she thought maybe you got a ride home with "some guy". I thought they could give me the number of the house where the party was but it was Jim Webber who informed me they don't have phones at gravel pits. That's a nice venue for a party of young people. I suppose they had one of those big kegs of beer too. I didn't ask Jim that because he was pretty peeved at being woken up. I mean… God forbid I should call earlier, embarrass my child, make her feel like a mummy's girl. Or how did you put it…like a "bug in a cage". God forbid that I should worry about my only child, the most precious thing I have left in the whole world. God forbid that I should worry, wondering if she's lying in a ditch somewhere, dead—

ELOISE: Stop it.

GLENN: Stop what? Caring? Loving you? I was two minutes away from calling the police. Where have you been? I want an answer and the answer had better be good.

ELOISE: OK!

    Pause.

I told Liz that I wanted a ride and then suddenly she and your precious Kevin had left and they hadn't even told me. I was right there.

GLENN: So, who did you leave with?

ELOISE: Gerry Little.

GLENN: On his four wheeler?!

ELOISE: Yes but I didn't even—

GLENN: How did Liz know that you left with him?

ELOISE: Because I called her on your cell. Later.

GLENN: But you couldn't call me?!

ELOISE: Because I knew you'd be all pissed off.

    GLENN notices the rip on ELOISE's dress.

GLENN: What's happened to your dress?

    GLENN leans to see the rip. ELOISE moves away.

Your knees are covered in dirt. What have you…?

Oh my lord. Oh my lord. Oh Ellie. Please don't tell me—

ELOISE: I didn't do anything! I didn't do *anything*!

GLENN: Then where have you been?!!

Pause.

Have you been drinking? Because if you have... Let me smell your breath.

ELOISE: No.

GLENN: Don't you say no to me. Breathe out.

ELOISE pushes her breath in her mother's face with a "hah".

Walk a straight line.

ELOISE considers if she will do this. Then does it, easily, back and forth back and forth, full of hostility.

ELOISE: Can I go to bed now?

GLENN: NO! Not until you tell me exactly what you have been doing.

ELOISE: Why should I tell you when you just told me you aren't going to believe me anyway! You've already made me feel like a jerk. Sometimes I think you would prefer it if I *was* lying dead in a ditch. It would justify you thinking I am a complete loser.

GLENN: Don't say that!

ELOISE: Why shouldn't I? That's how you make me feel.

GLENN: You know why I worry? You know why? Because sometimes I don't trust your judgment.

ELOISE: Oh. There. You see? Well at least you've admitted it.

GLENN: I don't trust your judgment because I had poor judgment at your age too. I got rides with boys I shouldn't have. Boys that had been drinking. I know it happens and I know awful accidents—

ELOISE: Well that's how we are different isn't it? Because, actually, I do have good judgment. I got on the four wheeler with Gerry. But before we had gone about five meters I figured out he'd been drinking and I made him let me off.

Pause.

GLENN: Then what happened?

ELOISE: *(Scoffing laugh.)*

GLENN: Did he follow you? Did he hurt you?

ELOISE: No.

GLENN: How did you get home?

ELOISE: I walked.

GLENN: The whole way?

ELOISE: Yes. If you want proof you can look at the sores on my feet.

GLENN: Why is your dress ripped?

ELOISE: I tripped…I swear!

GLENN: But if you left at midnight you should have been here at least an hour ago.

Pause.

There's something you're not telling me.

Pause.

Tell me.

Pause.

I promise I won't get angry.

ELOISE: Yeah right.

GLENN: I'm sorry. But I've been absolutely frantic. Can you think of this from my point of view, you said you'd be home by midnight and here it is almost—

ELOISE: You will never believe me... Not in a million years.

GLENN: Try me.

Pause.

ELOISE: Don't say I didn't warn you...and don't interrupt.

GLENN sits down on the porch stairs and waits.

OK... We left just after midnight; once I figured Liz had left without me. I don't think Gerry had been drinking much but I wasn't sure so I just thought it was better. So when I got off he drives away in a huff, gunning the wheels like a jerk. And I didn't want to go back to the party and look like a loser and I didn't want to call cause I thought you'd be sleeping and was thinking it's not very far to walk, maybe a half an hour, I mean I'm not an expert on distances, so I start walking. And I'm walking and walking along the road... And it's completely dark and my feet are sore...but I'm hurrying along cause I know I'm late and I know how freaked out you'll be. But of course it's taking way longer than I thought... And then I see these lights a ways off, coming behind me, you know how you can see a couple of clicks down the road? So I shift to the side because I don't know who's out driving around at that time of night and I don't want to be hit or have some yucky-stranger ask me if I want a ride. But the lights are coming fast and I get this idea that maybe it's Gerry, really pissed off. So I deke behind some trees. Waiting for him to go by. But I'm keeping an eye out...because something doesn't look right... Those lights're too high off the road. I thought maybe it was one of those big stupid monster trucks with the big crazy wheels. Larry Delray had one, remember? But...there's no sound, no gravel sound, no engine sound. And one time it veers off, I mean right off the road, and doesn't go into the ditch or bounce or anything. Just keeps moving steady. And I am getting totally freaked 'cause I am in the middle of nowhere. The closest house is a ways off, but there's a light on. I think, OK, I am just going to duck into the corn. And when I peek out I see the light coming closer, fast and I realize... They're not headlights, this... isn't a car.]Everything in me says get away from it. So I start running through the corn, like a crazy person, towards the house. And I can't feel my sore feet or the corn whipping at me, I just know I've got to keep running. And I'm running and I'm running and I'm thinking I'm friggin' well going to join that stupid Running Club at school and get in shape if I get out of this corn alive. I'm moving pretty good... But then I feel the light, I don't even have to look. I know whatever it is, it's coming after me. It's turned off the road, following me...there's light all over my back like...beams of sunshine, bright and hot and it's not acting like normal light, cause it's coming around me, in front of me, wrapping around, like it wants to hold me. I don't want to turn around and see what ever it is. I *really* don't want to see. I just keep running and zigzagging but somehow it moves with me. And I'm crying and running and I...see the house up ahead. And I think if I can just make it there... If I can get inside. And shut the door behind me I'll be OK. And then I'm out of the corn and I'm in some tall grass and I can see the house clearly now and I'm screaming for help and then...

> *ELOISE pauses. She looks at her mother who stands up, moving towards her...*

GLENN: What next, Eloise.

ELOISE: I tripped on something. Some old...stump or something and I go flying and...I can't move.

GLENN: What do you mean you can't move?

ELOISE: I can't move! I can't move my legs or my arms or anything. Something is stopping me from moving. Something is controlling my muscles. And I'm lying a bit on my side. So I can see out of the corner of my eye.

GLENN: See what?

ELOISE: The lights!

GLENN: I don't understand about the—

ELOISE: They were like nothing I've ever seen before. Light is the wrong word, they were...moving...floating, above the ground and—

> *GLENN slaps ELOISE across the face.*

GLENN: You must take me for a fool.

> *GLENN exits into the house. She goes right up the stairs. ELOISE stands, shocked and hurt. Eventually hurt turns to anger and it looks like ELOISE will walk away from the house...but a rustling in the corn stops her, frightens her...and she quickly goes into the house, locks the back door, turns out the back porch light and stands in the dark.*

Scene 3

The next morning. Nobody is around. CHRISTINE Clark, 24, appears. CHRISTINE is very modern looking with bright red hair. She has an air of confidence, sophistication. CHRISTINE knocks on the screen door. She waits. She knocks again. She waits.

CHRISTINE: Hello? Hello?

CHRISTINE looks around a little bit. Then she takes a cigarette out of her bag and lights it. She stands there, smoking and waiting a moment before walking away. After a beat or two we see Ellie sneaking downstairs . She looks very wary, trying to see who it was that knocked. ELOISE is in her PJs, a comforter wrapped around her. She slowly makes her way to the door, watching CHRISTINE walk away. When she is certain that CHRISTINE has gone ELOISE relaxes. She notices a note from her mother on the table. She reads it and makes a sound of derision at its contents. ELOISE walks to a cupboard and searches it before taking out a bag of Cheezies which she rips open and sits down to eat. After a moment she licks the orange cheese dust off her fingers, finds the phone and dials.

ELOISE: It's me... Yeah, I'm OK... Sorry I called so late last night, I had to call someone... No I'm alright. It was pretty weird though—I just— I know—of course she would call all in a panic. I can't believe she woke up your dad. He must have freaked... Well you should never have ditched me at that party! You knew I wanted a ride. I didn't even want to go but you said... OK. OK... Alright, already, don't get all twisted. I'm just calling to make sure you don't tell anybody... About what happened to me! Especially not Kevin, he's such a blabbermouth... No!... Well make sure he doesn't tell anybody or— ...Liz I mean it. I really, really mean it... You didn't tell anyone else did you?... I don't really know what happened anyway. I could have been a bit drunk or something... How do you know? Anyway, it's all a blur. I just know that— ...OK. I'll see you—

Liz isn't on the other end anymore Ellie hangs up..)

CHRISTINE: Hello.

CHRISTINE has come round the other side of the house and is looking in a window.

ELOISE: *(Gasps.)*

CHRISTINE: I'm sorry, did I scare you? *(Laughs.)* I didn't mean to. I knocked earlier so I didn't think anyone was home.

ELOISE: Then what are you doing looking in the window?

CHRISTINE: Waiting for someone to be home.

ELOISE: My mother's not here right now. Come back later.

CHRISTINE: Eloise. It's me, Christine Clark. Remember? I was your camp counsellor a few summers back? At that nature camp in the park.

ELOISE: That was ages ago. I was about six.

CHRISTINE: You were so cute. We caught the frogs and made them a home. Don't you remember?

ELOISE: Oh yeah...you look different.

CHRISTINE: I must look like an idiot standing outside here. I'll come round.

> *CHRISTINE disappears. ELOISE hurries to hide the Cheezies, wipes her mouth, fixes her hair, buttons up her PJs, wraps the comforter around her waist. CHRISTINE appears at the back door. She tries the screen door but it's hooked.*

Oops.

> *ELOISE unlocks the door. CHRISTINE enters.*

Is your mum still working at the post office?

ELOISE: Yeah. She'll be back after two.

CHRISTINE: I was really sorry to hear about your dad.

ELOISE: Yeah.

CHRISTINE: That must have been hard.

ELOISE: Yeah.

CHRISTINE: My mum told me. I remember he used to pick you up from the camp. He was so nice. He let you take the frog home that day, remember?

ELOISE: I guess so.

CHRISTINE: You called the frog Tybalt. I'll never forget that. What ever happened to old Tybalt?

ELOISE: We put him in the culvert. I think a car ran over him about two days later and he was shmushed.

> *Pause.*

Would you like some water or something?

CHRISTINE: Sure, that would be nice. Thanks.

> *ELOISE gets CHRISTINE a glass of water.*

Who's doing the farm work?

ELOISE: Mum's renting out the fields to the Thoms. I want her to sell but she won't.

CHRISTINE: It's so funny to see all the kids I worked with all grown up now. It makes me feel so old. I come home in the summer and I don't recognize half of them. They're the only thing that ever changes around here.

ELOISE: Where are you living now?

CHRISTINE: Kingston, going to Queens. I couldn't wait to get out. I felt completely suffocated. I only came back because I got a job for my co-op component. Sorry, I know you live here...maybe you don't feel that way...but I hate being in a place where everybody is discussing everybody's business; so-and-so's facial hair or so-and-so's bad choice of lawn furniture... it's so small-minded.

ELOISE: Yeah.

CHRISTINE: I mean the looks I get about my hair. No one would look twice at me at Queens. Do you know what I mean?

ELOISE: Yeah...I guess so.

CHRISTINE: I never fit in here. Well soon enough I won't have to ever come back. What are you going to do when you graduate?

ELOISE: I don't know yet. Maybe go into early childhood education.

CHRISTINE: You'd be good at that.

                Pause.

               I guess you're wondering why I'm here.

ELOISE: Yeah, well...kinda.

CHRISTINE: I just came on a whim. I'm not keeping you from anything am I?

ELOISE: Uh...I should probably get dressed.

CHRISTINE: Oh I love it that you're still in your pyjamas and it's almost noon. Reminds me of my own wayward youth. Don't worry...I won't stay long...

              ELOISE sits.

              I'm just going to get right to the point... Did you see something strange last night?

ELOISE: ...No... Why, did you?

CHRISTINE: Now I feel completely ridiculous. I think I'd better tell you where I am coming from.

ELOISE: OK.

CHRISTINE: You've probably heard already. About the thing I saw?

ELOISE: No.

CHRISTINE: Huh... That's funny. I thought everyone knew.

ELOISE: I really have no idea what you are talking about.

CHRISTINE: OK.

              Pause.

              When my family first moved here we lived in this big old heritage farmhouse towards Wingham. Way off the road. Nothing but corn for hectares and hectares. Couldn't even see the closest barn.

ELOISE: Kinda like this place?

CHRISTINE: The house was a bit nicer. My parents wanted peace and quiet or something ridiculous. I was about ten, I guess, and my brother and sister were a bit younger. I never liked the house one bit. It had this really weird feeling about it. But nobody else felt it. We'd moved here from Oshawa and I found all the country sounds strange at first so I thought maybe it was all just in my head. But...whenever I was alone in the house I heard things. A child crying. Weeping. Softly. Real sad. Always coming from one room. An upstairs bedroom. The plaster was coming off in there so we just stored things in that room. I didn't like to go near it but one time the door was jammed and my mum was trying to get in to get some game my brother wanted and she called my father and he couldn't get it open and for some reason I knew I would be able to open it so I did. I just opened it. Turned the door knob. Easy as pie. My mum and dad couldn't believe it. I made sure I was never in the house by myself, ever. They got me a dog, a big Shepherd trying to make me feel safer but...I kept hearing this crying. It was so sad and lonely. You know? Then one night Mum and Dad went out. I pleaded with them not to but they said they had to get away sometimes and they got me a babysitter. Jeanette her name was I think. I liked her because she thought the house was creepy too. My parents left in the car and as soon as we all walked back into the house the crying started; a little girl, clear as day, calling..."Mama...Mama..." And I'm standing at the bottom of the stairs, and that great big Shepherd dog starts whimpering and cowering...and I hear the door to the upstairs bedroom open, all by itself. Creaks open. And this girl appears, at the top of the stairs. In an old-fashioned dress. And she reaches out to me, and says..."Where's Mama?" And the door to the bedroom starts banging and banging and banging. Like it was angry. I bolted outside and took off down the road, I was totally freaking out, with Jeanette, the dog, my brother and sister running after me. I point-blank refused to go back in there.

We had to walk into town to call my mum and dad. I screamed so loud we had to stay at a motel. And Mum and Dad had to sell the house.

Pause.

You know why I'm telling you this don't you?

ELOISE: No.

CHRISTINE: I always wondered. Why did she just appear to me? Was I special? Did I have some kind of sight?… You saw something last night, didn't you? Something out of the ordinary.

ELOISE: I didn't see any little girls in old-fashioned dresses.

CHRISTINE: What did you see?

ELOISE: I really don't know what you are talking about.

CHRISTINE: Kevin Webber told me you saw something strange.

ELOISE: He's such a liar.

CHRISTINE: Why would he make that up?

ELOISE: Because I called Liz and told her that's what I was going to tell my mum. To get out of trouble for being late.

CHRISTINE: Liz said you were hysterical and crying for help.

ELOISE: She told you that?

CHRISTINE: Yes she did. Just this morning.

ELOISE: I had a couple of drinks. It was late and I was lost so I was scared. It wasn't a big deal.

CHRISTINE: I wondered if that was the case but Liz also says you don't drink.

ELOISE: Oh she did, did she? What else did she tell you? My whole life story?

CHRISTINE: She thinks you were telling the truth. She thinks you saw something bizarre near the Burns line.

ELOISE: Oh yeah. If she's so sure I was telling the truth then why didn't she help me? I mean did she tell you that?

CHRISTINE: I don't know what motivates Liz exactly but I think Liz mostly thinks about Liz.

ELOISE: Why should I tell you anything? I don't really even know you.

CHRISTINE: You don't have to tell me anything if you don't want to but...I guess, I just have a need to know... that there are things out there... That every question can't be answered; there's not always an explanation that fits the mould. Y'now?

Pause.

What did you see, Eloise?

ELOISE: This is weird. I think you had better go.

CHRISTINE: OK. Alright. It was totally presumptuous of me to come. I was just thinking how I felt, how what had happened to me was so extraordinary. But I felt all alone because no one would listen.

ELOISE stays quiet. CHRISTINE makes like she is going to leave.

ELOISE: It wasn't a ghost. I don't want you thinking that I'm seeing ghosts.

CHRISTINE: And what would be wrong with that?

ELOISE: I don't know what I saw. It was late and dark and...I was scared.

CHRISTINE: You were over on Burns line?

ELOISE: Somewhere west of Harlock I think.

CHRISTINE: And?

ELOISE: It was like a big glowy light. Hovering above the ground.

CHRISTINE: How big?

ELOISE: Big. But it kept changing so… It followed me off the road into a corn field.

CHRISTINE: Then what happened?

ELOISE: I was running away from it and I tripped and I couldn't move. And this light just kind of… floated…about fifteen feet away. Not making sound at all but there was a rushing, like a huge wind, blowing my face and my hair, whooshing through the corn, like a hurricane was coming.

CHRISTINE: Did you see anybody?

ELOISE: No. But I could feel something. I could feel eyes on me.

CHRISTINE: (Softly.) Oh my God.

ELOISE: Watching me. Studying me. Like something was absorbing me completely.

Pause.

CHRISTINE: Go on.

ELOISE: There was a dog barking like crazy and running towards me, coming to protect me. It came right up to me and barked at this light. Yap yap yap. I'm sure whatever it was wasn't scared of the dog but it seemed to break the spell, you know? I could move. I could crawl away, out of the light and when I turned to have a really good look—it was moving away. Fast. Like a shooting star. Only instead of falling down it was moving up, into the sky…and it was gone. And the wind stopped. I could hear the dog yapping and the crickets and…my heart was pounding like it was going to burst out of my friggin' body.

CHRISTINE: What did you do?

ELOISE: I ran to the house and banged on the door. Over and over. Really loud. I tried the door. It was locked. Nobody was home. I hid behind a chair, on the porch, with the dog. I called Liz on my cell phone, I don't know what I expected… The dog was sweet. One of those mutts, you know? He even walked me partway home.

CHRISTINE: Do you think it left any signs?

ELOISE: Like what?

CHRISTINE: What do you think it was?

ELOISE: I don't know.

CHRISTINE: If you had to classify it…I mean, you sound pretty certain that it wasn't a ghost—could it have been a different kind of poltergeist? A spirit of some kind?

ELOISE: I don't think so.

CHRISTINE: Maybe it was some kind of vision.

ELOISE: A vision of what?

CHRISTINE: Or…do you think it was a UFO?

ELOISE: It certainly was unidentified.

CHRISTINE: Maybe a space ship?

ELOISE: You mean like a flying saucer? No.

CHRISTINE: Something from another world though.

ELOISE: Well, it wasn't from any world I know.

CHRISTINE: Then maybe there are signs of it, marks on the ground or—

ELOISE: Proof? Why don't you ask the dog? *(Laugh.)* You know the grass probably would show something. It was tall and that wind would have flattened it for sure.

CHRISTINE: Which house was it?

ELOISE: I don't know. I wasn't really paying attention. I was scared out of my gourd.

CHRISTINE: I don't blame you.

> *CHRISTINE stands.*

What an incredible experience.

ELOISE: You probably think I'm nuts.

CHRISTINE: No I don't. Besides do you really care what people think?

ELOISE: Yeah.

CHRISTINE: It's funny. When you get out in the real world, away from this small town stuff, all those things you thought were so important…aren't really. I used to be obsessed with blending in. And now that I'm at university I want to stand out.

ELOISE: Right now blending is just fine with me.

CHRISTINE: You'll be OK. One day you'll thank me.

ELOISE: For what?

CHRISTINE: For believing you.

Scene 4

> *GLENN is in the kitchen making breakfast. She pours ELOISE orange juice. The phone rings.*

GLENN: Hello?...Hey Bobbie, what's up? Did Ellie call you about her birthday?... Oh my Lord, I told her last week to— ...I don't know what she wants to do. I can't seem to talk to her. She just... No. I just got up. I'm making breakfast. Why? What day is it today? Wednesday?...Geez I'm losing my marbles, I don't think I even picked up the mail... Alright...I'll go and get it right now. Does Jane have one of her recipes in again? I made that thing with the marshmallows and completely ruined my new frying pan... OK, OK... I'll call you back.

> *She calls upstairs.*

Ellie. Time to get up. It's getting late. Ellie!

> *ELOISE groans offstage.*

Don't go back to sleep. I'm going to grab yesterday's mail.

> *GLENN leaves out the door. After a moment ELOISE comes down in her usual sluggish manner and pours the orange juice down the sink before she starts making her breakfast. GLENN returns holding the local paper. She stops on the porch to leaf through it. An article attracts her attention. She reads it for a moment before:*

Oh, my, heavens...Ellie!

ELOISE: What?

GLENN: Come here.

ELOISE: I'm eating my breakfast.

            GLENN keeps reading for a bit.

GLENN: When did you talk to Christine Clark?

            Pause.

ELOISE: Why?

GLENN: Come here right now.

            ELOISE comes out onto the porch.

            I don't believe this.

ELOISE: What?…What? !

GLENN: Did you speak to her? Did you say all that?

ELOISE: Did I say what?

GLENN: What were you thinking, telling her all that
            nonsense about the other night.

            *She thrusts the article in front of ELOISE. ELOISE
            glances at it.*

ELOISE: She's a reporter?

GLENN: You knew that. I told you ages ago. She came
            home from whatever university she's been taking
            journalism at…to work at the *Clarion*. Miss Big
            Town girl now, thinking she's better than all of us.
            Her mother always let her run wild—

ELOISE: I don't remember you telling me anything.

GLENN: You don't listen.

ELOISE: I didn't know she was a reporter. She just dropped
            by and started asking me questions. She never once
            said—

GLENN: She came here, to the house? That really takes the cake. That girl has always been a liar. Did you tell her this story?

ELOISE: I don't know. I haven't even read it.

GLENN: Read away.

ELOISE sits down to read for a moment before...

ELOISE: Oh my god... She's twisted my words! She's making it sound like I said I saw some big UFO with blinking lights and everything. I never said that.

GLENN: Look...everything you say is in quotation marks.

ELOISE: But I didn't say that! Not exactly that anyway. Or... but—

GLENN: *(Reads.)* "...however no corroborating proof was found. This reporter asked every resident on Burns line within a mile of Harlock about that evening. No one had heard or seen anything out of the ordinary. Not one out-of-place blade of grass was found. " So that pretty much seals it.

ELOISE: I sound like a goof. Everybody is going think I'm a complete freak.

GLENN: First of all, you had better learn to think before you go blabbing some wild story all over town.

ELOISE: She tricked me. She told me a whole thing about how she had seen a ghost and—

GLENN: She told you about that poor little phantom girl crying for her mummy? I've heard so many versions of that baloney—

ELOISE: She told me she believed me and now...she sounds like she's making fun of me—

GLENN: Believed you? Believed you saw a flying saucer?

ELOISE: I never said I saw a flying saucer! I never said that.

GLENN: You told me you saw floating lights that pinned you to the ground! I mean really Ellie, if this is a cry for attention it's going a bit too far.

ELOISE: I didn't know she was going to print it the in damned paper!

GLENN: Watch your language or you'll go to your room for a week! There is no need to—

ELOISE: Fine. I'll happily go to my room for the rest of my life and never come out.

               ELOISE furiously rips up the paper into small pieces.

GLENN: You're going to go to school this morning. I'll drive you—

ELOISE: No, I'm not. You can call and say I've got stomach flu. I am not walking in there and have everyone look at me like I'm a freak.

GLENN: Oh yes you will. Because that's what I have to do. I'll be facing the whole town today, coming in to buy stamps. And then asking me if my daughter is spending time with little green men.

ELOISE: Oh this is all about you is it? This is all about your embarrassment. How this will reflect on you. Of course, even when Dad was dying it was all about you wasn't it?

               Pause.

GLENN: You can be very cruel some times. Do you know that?

ELOISE: So can you.

               Pause.

GLENN: Eloise. You didn't take any drugs at that party, did you?

ELOISE: *(Groaning.)* Ahhh… Of course not.

GLENN: Then tell me what really happened.

ELOISE: Alright. I took a ride with Gerry Little. We spent hours groping each other in a field of soy beans. Is that what you want to hear?

GLENN: You're impossible. I don't know what to do with you.

    The phone rings.

    That will be your Aunty Bobbie. Who wants to do something nice for your birthday. You didn't even call her back.

ELOISE: I forgot.

GLENN: Well, maybe if you thought about anybody but your self you'd have remembered.

    GLENN goes in to answer the phone.

    Sorry Bobby, I just got— …Just a minute, please… It's for you.

    ELOISE comes inside.

ELOISE: Hello? …Who is this?…

    ELOISE hangs up the phone looking stricken.

GLENN: What? Who was it?

    ELOISE is considering what to say when the phone rings again. GLENN picks it up.

    Hello?… Who is this?… Tell me who this…

    She hangs up. A moment later the phone starts

*ringing and ringing… GLENN finally walks over
to the telephone charger and unplugs it.*

ELOISE: If you think I am going to go back to that school,
you are going to have to pick me up and drag me
there. I will never, ever…

*ELOISE runs up to her room and slams the door
shut. After a moment GLENN speaks to an unseen
being.*

GLENN: I don't want to hear anything from you. Oh yes I
can feel your eyes upon me. Watching me mess up
everything. Why don't you come down here and
tell me yourself, huh, if you think you can do the job
better. Stop sitting up there in judgment and help
me.

Blackout.

End of Act One.

Act Two

Scene 5

One week later. Over the course of this scene the sun goes down slowly until it is dark. There are piles of dishes in the kitchen—ELOISE's mess from the day. The back door has a sign pinned on it reading "TAKE ME TO YOUR LEADER". After a moment we hear a car drive up. It's GLENN returning home carrying groceries. She looks at the door and sighs. She goes inside. She puts down the groceries and calls upstairs.

GLENN: Ellie! I'm home.

ELOISE: *(Off.)* Congratulations!

GLENN: Can you come down here? I need to talk to you.

ELOISE: *(Off.)* Just a minute.

GLENN notices the mess. She calls up again.

GLENN: Ellie, please come down here. Right now. This kitchen looks like a tornado hit it.

GLENN starts puts groceries away until Ellie comes down in her PJs.)

ELOISE: What?

GLENN: *(Indicating door.)* Did you see this?

ELOISE nods.

Look at this mess. Don't you know how to wash a dish? Help me out now.

> *GLENN starts to clean up. ELOISE helps half heartedly under:*

Did anyone call?

ELOISE: I don't know. I turned the ringer off.

GLENN: Listen. Tell me. What are your long term plans? To stay home in your pyjamas for the rest of your life and eat Cheezies?

ELOISE: Maybe.

GLENN: Because, my dear, at some point you're going to have to come to terms with this situation. Face your demons and make peace with whatever you've done.

> *Pause, then calmer.*

You need to look inside yourself and decide how you are going to deal with this. I have indulged you staying home for almost a week because I know this is difficult for you but it seems the situation is not getting any better. We all have our crosses to bear and yours is no greater than—

ELOISE: You haven't been talking to Reverend Mathews have you?

GLENN: Yes, I spoke to him today as—

ELOISE: Did you have a little chat about me?

GLENN: Yes. I did.

ELOISE: I can't believe it.

GLENN: Well who do you want me to talk to? The whole town is looking at me funny. The girls at work are such gossips I can't talk to them. I've talked Aunty Bobie's ear off—

ELOISE: So what did the Pastor have to say?

GLENN: He was very nice. He said that people, especially young people, say things for different reasons. That one must be patient and understanding but also give guidance so they know to do the right thing. And eventually the truth will come forth.

ELOISE: And what exactly is the right thing that will make the truth come forth?

GLENN: That's something only you can know.

ELOISE: Oh. Right. That answer. I really, really hate that answer.

GLENN: Because it forces you to actually confront your problems.

ELOISE: Why is everybody making such a big deal about this? Why won't they leave me alone?

GLENN: Because you are making a big deal about it, staying at home, hiding your head in a hole.

ELOISE: So Reverend Mathews thinks I'm a freak.

GLENN: No he doesn't. He's heard a lot of things in his time, not much fazes him.

ELOISE: He probably thinks I got a visitation from God or something.

Pause.

GLENN: Ellie. Could that… Is that a possibility?

ELOISE: No!

GLENN: Don't rule it out. I knew a woman who used to see

God in her barn on a regular basis and she was one
of the sanest women I ever met.

ELOISE: And what did God look like?

GLENN: I don't know. I never asked her.

ELOISE: Would that make you feel better? If I saw God
instead of something else.

GLENN: Well.

ELOISE: How is seeing God better? I mean all these people
believe in God and they don't have any proof
positive of that.

GLENN: Ellie. The things that come out of your mouth are
incredible sometimes. You should stop and listen to
yourself.

ELOISE: Stop and listen to yourself. I hear you talking to
God all the time. Out loud. Like he's right there.

GLENN: I do not.

ELOISE: You do so. I can hear you as clear as anything. You
stand right under my window, yakking away to
God like he's right there.

GLENN: Ellie stop.

ELOISE: Oh I see. I'm the freak because I saw some lights
that can't be explained but it's OK for you to—

GLENN: I am not talking to God.

ELOISE: Then who are you talking to?

GLENN: It's complicated.

ELOISE: You don't want to tell me, do you?

GLENN: Eloise.

ELOISE: Then who is it, some imaginary friend? Some little fairy or a green elf who—

GLENN: Stop it… I am talking to your father.

ELOISE: To Dad? Can you see him? Is he like a ghost?

GLENN: No! Of course not. Nothing like that. But sometimes… *(Laughs.)* You must think I am losing my marbles. I'm sure it's just wishful thinking, or maybe we were just together so long but… sometimes it feels like he is right there, I can even smell that shaving soap he liked to use.

ELOISE: You think *I'm* weird.

GLENN: I love you so much, Ellie. I do. I may not show it all the time, I know that I come across as hard but really I'm just doing my best.

ELOISE: I know.

GLENN: You seem so angry with me all the time.

> *Pause.*

Are you?

ELOISE: No. Not all the time.

GLENN: What are you angry about?

ELOISE: You don't want to know.

GLENN: I do. Tell me.

ELOISE: Why did you stop going to see Dad in the hospital?

> *Pause.*

GLENN: Is that what this is about? All this anger?

ELOISE: Just give me an answer and then I'll know.

GLENN: Oh my...Ellie...you think I don't have my own guilt? I punish myself every day.

ELOISE: Is that why you talk to him?

GLENN: He told me not to come.

ELOISE: I don't believe it.

GLENN: I found it very hard to keep it together; every time I had to hold that vomit dish or see him in such pain—I'd be a basket case, and he didn't like it. I really tried not to show it but—

ELOISE: It wasn't about you, it was about him. He needed us.

GLENN: And I need him here every second of every day. People keep telling me it's going to get easier but it doesn't. It gets harder and harder. Especially when I have a daughter who looks like she wishes it was me buried in the cemetery. And there are some days I wish it *was* the other way around. I know he could have helped you better. But you're stuck with me. For now... Until you leave me too.

ELOISE: Who said I'm going to leave you?

GLENN: You'll go away to school the minute you get a chance and that'll be that. And I'll be fifty years old and all on my own. Maybe you'll be home for Christmas or Thanksgiving if I'm lucky, but basically I will be alone.

ELOISE: Don't get so morbid.

GLENN: Just you wait. You have your whole life ahead of you and... I'm gearing up for the final act.

ELOISE: Mother. Stop.

GLENN: I have buried my husband. I'm going through menopause, which is your body saying " See that face in the mirror? Those wrinkles aren't going anyplace but down. Those aches and pains you feel aren't going to get any better."

Pause.

We wanted to have more children... Your dad and I...but for some reason I couldn't. Part of God's plan I guess.

Pause.

ELOISE: Maybe you'll meet someone else.

GLENN: What men am I going to meet around here? Mr. Gibbs from the hardware store? Every time he lectures me about the proper care and storage of my tools I realize there's a good reason he's single.

ELOISE: Oh come on now. He's nice. And he looks so handsome with his greased back hair. What does he use? Raccoon fat?

GLENN: *(Laughing.)* Stop.

ELOISE: I'm not going to leave you. I am not even ever going to leave this house.

GLENN: You're going to have to eventually.

ELOISE: Nope. I'm just going to lie low. I'm going to lie so low that one day I'll just blend in with the horizon and I won't be that girl who was in the science club. Who looks like a dork when she plays soccer. Who liked Shakespeare. Whose father died. The weirdo who saw something from outer space.

Pause.

GLENN: How are we going to deal with this? You have to go back to school.

ELOISE: Why? Can't I home-school?

GLENN: Are you joking? With me teaching you math? I
            don't even know what an integer is. I have never
            been a home-school type of mother and I never will
            be.

ELOISE: I can change schools.

GLENN: Come on. Think practically. You may not like what
            Reverend Mathews has to say but he's right.

ELOISE: No matter what I do it will be the wrong thing!

GLENN: OK now. Listen. We can figure this out. You really
            believe you saw something that night.

ELOISE: Yes. But I don't know what.

GLENN: OK. But...what if... I mean it was late and dark and
            your imagination plays games with you. Years ago
            there were folks somewhere in the States. It was all
            over the papers that they had seen flying saucers.
            Some kid had even taken pictures of the saucers
            streaking across the sky. Well they trotted out all the
            best scientists to look at the pictures and you know
            what they turned out to be?

ELOISE: What?

GLENN: Plovers. A flock of birds. The way the light hit
            them they looked like flying saucers but it was just
            plovers.

ELOISE: I didn't see a bunch of birds.

GLENN: Remember when the Murphys rented a big
            spotlight for Marion's sixtieth? Could it have been
            something like that?

ELOISE: I don't think so.

GLENN: It's just not possible that you saw something or
            someone...from another planet. They don't exist.

People have been trying to prove that stuff for years and they haven't had any luck.

ELOISE: Well I don't know what I saw. I saw something.

GLENN: OK, then, Eloise, what do you want people to believe you saw? Do you want them to believe you saw some supernatural phantom? I mean, most won't and then where will you be?

Pause. GLENN notices the time.

Now, you think about it. Christine Clark will be here any minute and you want to make sure you have your story straight.

ELOISE: What are you talking about? Christine Clark?

GLENN: I just told you she was coming. You didn't register it because we got side-tracked on to something else.

ELOISE: You did not tell me that.

GLENN: I'm sure I told you. I've got so much in my head I can't seem to keep it all straight.

ELOISE: You asked her to come here, after what she wrote about me?

GLENN: I'm sorry, I meant to tell you properly.

ELOISE: Did you go and see her?

GLENN: I was walking by the *Clarion* offices and I thought—

ELOISE: You've been really busy haven't you? Going to see the Pastor. Going to see Christine Clark. What's next? The friggin' psychiatrist? Going to get me locked up in the loony bin?

Noticing time.

GLENN: Good grief, help me clean this up or she'll be writing about my lack of housekeeping skills.

ELOISE: I'm not talking to her.

GLENN: Ellie… This is your chance to set it right.

ELOISE: Don't touch me!

GLENN: Just listen for once. I thought maybe…that if she came here…you could tell her it was a mistake and she could write a retraction.

ELOISE: You've got it all figured out, don't you? What am I going to say to her? That I was lying?

GLENN: No. Just say you're not sure what you saw. It was an optical illusion, it was dark, maybe you hit your head when you tripped and fell. Then you can go back to school and it may be hard for a couple of days but then it will be over and people will forget all about it. You'll get through it. You've got through worse.

              Sound of car pulling up. Car door opening and shutting, footsteps on gravel…under:

              I'm only trying to do what's right for you. I only want to see you happy.

              ELOISE runs upstairs and slams her door. CHRISTINE knocks. GLENN opens the door for her.

CHRISTINE: Hi, Mrs. Bernhardt.

GLENN: Thanks for coming Christine. Sorry about the mess.

CHRISTINE: That's OK. I hate clean houses. They make me nervous.

GLENN: Good. Then you'll feel right at home. Would you like a cup of tea?

CHRISTINE: Have you got coffee?

GLENN: Decaf? I've got instant.

CHRISTINE: Instant decaf? I'd rather drink sewer water. I've got a deadline and I'm going to be up writing all night.

GLENN: Caffeinated it is then.

> *GLENN starts to make coffee.*

CHRISTINE: I got a scoop on that Goderich girl who's signed the big modeling contract.

> *Pause.*

So Ellie wants to change her story?

GLENN: She's been thinking about that night.

CHRISTINE: I hear she hasn't been feeling well.

GLENN: Quite frankly she's having a hard time with the whole thing.

CHRISTINE: She knows it's just journalism right? What sells papers. We sold every paper we printed last week.

GLENN: I don't think a fifteen-year-old girl is interested in circulation numbers.

CHRISTINE: She's feisty. She'll be OK.

GLENN: She's been through a lot this last year. She doesn't feel OK.

CHRISTINE: Did you ask me to come out here to make me feel pissy? Because I can defend what I wrote. I didn't write anything that she didn't say. I checked it out. I drove up and down Burns line and knocked on every house. Everyone was home that night. Nobody saw any strange lights. She told me she banged on the door of a house. Banged on it loud and clear yet nobody heard anything. I looked at every corn field, every lawn and blade of grass. No sign of anything. I believed what she told me. But when I didn't find one shred of evidence... I was just doing my job.

GLENN: So you think she made it up.

CHRISTINE: I don't make the judgments. I just report the story. It's everyone else who comes to their own conclusions.

GLENN: I didn't ask you out here to make you feel "pissy" as you say. But perhaps you could take pity and let her tell her side of it. With some dignity.

CHRISTINE: I'm not going to retract what I said. No matter how many dirty looks that snoopy Mrs. Barber gives me. And I am certainly not going to be guilted into writing some feel-good follow-up.

GLENN: You're not writing for the *Washington Post*. You are a fourth year journalism student with a co-op placement at a local paper. Who didn't even tell the person she was interviewing that she was a reporter.

CHRISTINE: You don't tell everyone that. I didn't hide it either. She didn't ask.

GLENN: Give her a break will you? Her father died of cancer less than a year ago. She's having trouble at school. And now she won't leave the house.

CHRISTINE: OK!

GLENN: Alright!

                Pause.

              How do you take your coffee?

CHRISTINE: Black.

Pause.

So where is she?

GLENN: Up in her room.

CHRISTINE: She doesn't even want to talk to me, does she? This is your brilliant idea. You know, maybe this is not such a smart move.

> *ELOISE's door opens and ELOISE comes down the stairs. She is dressed, with her hair combed and neat.*

Hey... Eloise.

> *Pause. GLENN gives CHRISTINE her coffee.*

Thanks.

ELOISE: I want to talk to Christine alone.

GLENN: I think I should stay.

CHRISTINE: You afraid I'm going to twist her arm or something?

GLENN: No. Just her words.

ELOISE: I'll be alright Mum.

GLENN: OK. I'll be in the living room if you need me.

> *GLENN exits.*

CHRISTINE: So...do you hate me?

ELOISE: Something like that.

CHRISTINE: I wanted to believe you. Honestly I did. I bent over backwards looking for one single thing to back up your story.

ELOISE: And what evidence did you have of your ghost?

CHRISTINE: There was lots of evidence. But people chose to interpret things to their liking.

ELOISE: Right.

CHRISTINE: Listen. I know this was your mother's idea. If you don't want to talk that's OK.

ELOISE: No. I'm glad you came. Because I do want to set things straight.

CHRISTINE takes out a notebook and pencil.

CHRISTINE: OK. I'm listening.

ELOISE: Apparently it was a trick. I spoke to a friend just today and she said there are rumours flying all over school that someone played a joke on me.

CHRISTINE: Really?

ELOISE: It was a total set up. They made sure I was chased off the road at a certain place, they had the lights all ready.

CHRISTINE: You said the lights were hovering.

ELOISE: They had them hooked up in the trees so they were off the ground.

CHRISTINE: What about the wind?

ELOISE: It was windy that night. The wind probably helped move the lights around.

CHRISTINE: The dog and banging on the door?

ELOISE: I'm not even sure it was the Burns line. I didn't really have my bearings.

CHRISTINE: Who would play a trick like that?

ELOISE: Some jerk. Guys do it all the time. Friggin' Larry Delray once scared Janice out of her gourd by pretending he was an escaped convict.

CHRISTINE: Are you saying Larry might have done this?

ELOISE: I don't know but I wouldn't be surprised if he had something to do with it.

CHRISTINE: Who told you this "so called" rumour?

ELOISE: I don't want to say. I don't want you mixing up her words too.

CHRISTINE: Liz?

ELOISE: I'm not saying.

CHRISTINE: So you're suddenly changing your mind on this? Sounds a bit convenient to me.

ELOISE: It makes sense. It's totally believable... What? Do you honestly think I could have seen an alien spaceship? Give me a break. Or maybe you think everyone can see ghosts and goblins.

CHRISTINE: Alright... I'll write it up, see if I can make any kind of story out of it... Talk to your friend and see if you can get more details.

ELOISE: OK.

CHRISTINE starts to leave then stops.

CHRISTINE: You know... Everybody treated me like a freak. My parents thought I was nuts and took me to see some "specialist" in London who diagnosed me as having an overactive imagination. My brother and sister teased me relentlessly. Kids at school used to write horrible mean things on my desk. And that Halloween a group of them, about ten, showed up at our house covered with white sheets and cried "Mama, Mama" until my Dad threatened to call the police. In this town, I am still called a liar. And I always will be.

ELOISE: That's supposed to make me feel better?

CHRISTINE: But you know what? In the end it made me strong. I know what I saw and nobody can take that away from me. It makes me special. I don't base my self-evaluation on what others think of me. I know who I am.

ELOISE: Good for you.

CHRISTINE: I mean it. This will pass. You'll move on and won't even know what the fuss was about. *(Calling off.)* Good-bye Mrs. Bernhardt.

>	*CHRISTINE is out the door when GLENN comes in.*

GLENN: Good-bye, Christine. Did you two get things sorted out?

CHRISTINE: Thanks for the coffee.

GLENN: *(Calling off.)* You're welcome. Say hello to your mother for me.

>	*She watches CHRISTINE get into her car and drive down the road.*

You did the right thing.

ELOISE: I knew you were listening.

GLENN: I wouldn't put it past Larry Delray. He's always looking for new ways to make trouble. I think you are really wise. You can call your friends and get that story around and then you can be back at school day after tomorrow.

>	*They start cleaning up the kitchen. After a moment we hear a car approaching.*

GLENN: She's coming back. Did she forget something?

ELOISE: I don't see anything.

> *Sound of car door opening. GLENN goes outside to greet her.*

GLENN: *(Calling off.)* You journalists always have one more question to ask. *(To herself.)* Oh my goodness.

> *NIC Barlow appears. NIC is an attractive, smart looking man in his early thirties. He carries some books and papers.)*

Can I help you?

NIC: I hope you got my message.

ELOISE: *(Low.)* I forgot... I turned off the phone and never checked the messages.

GLENN: Oh my lord, of course, you must be Ellie's science teacher.

NIC: How'd you guess?

GLENN: Oh...well...I—

NIC: I'm Nic Barlow.

> *He puts his hand out and they shake hands.*

GLENN: Right.

NIC: I just wanted to drop off this assignment for Ellie.

GLENN: Oh. Of course.

NIC: Good to meet you Mrs. Bernhardt. I hope you don't mind me dropping by...it was on my way.

GLENN: No that's very kind of you. Call me Glenn. Do you want to come in? I'm afraid the house is an absolute mess.

NIC: Don't worry. Please. I won't stay long. I just have a few things to explain to Ellie. But we can sit out here. It's such a fantastic night. I just love these

	warm fall evenings. And I've been cooped up inside all day.
GLENN:	Alright. Of course. Ellie.

ELOISE comes out, making a face at her mother.

Well. I'll leave you two. I'll just be inside. Ellie, you call if you need anything.

GLENN goes inside, she stands in the kitchen, listening. After a moment she putters in the kitchen under:

NIC:	How's it going?
ELOISE:	It's going.
NIC:	You look like you're going to survive. I was beginning to worry that stomach flu was turning out to be a more serious illness.
ELOISE:	Well you know. It takes a bit to get your energy back.
NIC:	I'll bet it does. Hey. I passed that reporter woman on the way in. What's she up to now?
ELOISE:	Not much. Just some more questions.
NIC:	Yeah?
ELOISE:	Yeah.
NIC:	Is that good?
ELOISE:	I guess so.
NIC:	Come sit down. I've brought a bunch of stuff for you to catch up on; review sheets from the chemistry unit, pages to read from our favourite text book. Here's the list.

He hands her a page.

ELOISE: OK. And you have...some assignment?

NIC: Yup. Here's the stuff on that. There's a marking rubric that's pretty detailed. Look it over before you start.

          ELOISE looks over the paper.

ELOISE: Famous scientists?

          GLENN moves to the door to listen again. After a moment the phone rings. GLENN picks up the phone and moves to another room—all under:

NIC: Some famous, some not so famous. The criteria is that they had to have made a difference to how folks look at the world. There are three research components; the times they lived in and how they influenced their work; their major scientific discoveries and then how their discoveries were viewed by their peers and the general population. Finally I want you to be able get up in front of the class—give a short presentation, explain one of their theories and, you know, tell us your opinion about these guys, were they admirable, not so likeable and like that.

ELOISE: OK. Can I pick whoever I want?

NIC: I picked for you. Galileo Galilei.

ELOISE: Galileo. He's that Italian astronomer.

NIC: Also referred to as the father of modern astronomy, the father of modern physics and the father of science.

ELOISE: Sounds like he had a lot of kids.

NIC: Three actually. But all out of wedlock, even though he was a big time Catholic. Folks didn't like it but he really didn't think it was an issue. He was a big believer that you had to separate science from philosophy or religion. He believed that the laws of nature were mathematical and that the language of God is mathematics. Of course the Pope didn't agree with him on that one.

ELOISE: Isn't he the one that said the Earth moves around the sun?

NIC: Yeah. You know the guy. Actually it was Copernicus who came up with that concept. The Catholic church wasn't too keen on it. Their interpretation of the bible, back around 1600, was that the Earth is the centre of all things and everything moves around us. So then Copernicus comes up with this revolutionary idea.

ELOISE: Didn't Copernicus get in trouble for that?

NIC: Not so much. He didn't publish his theories until just before he died. So he escaped most of the bad stuff. And besides he was just a guy with an idea. Galileo offered the proof.

ELOISE: He invented the telescope didn't he?

NIC: Didn't invent it, but refined it. Made it powerful enough to see Jupiter and its moons for the first time. Must have been amazing. He saw the moons appearing and disappearing around Jupiter and figured the whole picture out. So Galileo starts shouting out that Copernicus was right. "Earth is moving around the immovable Sun!" Rotating and spinning at an incredible rate. I mean how can that be, why aren't we falling off? Falling over? The thought is dizzying. This was at a time that some poor monk was burned at the stake for exactly that kind of chat. I don't blame them actually, I'd probably have preferred to think of the Earth as just plain solid under my feet too.

ELOISE: He got stuff wrong though. He also said the tides were caused by the Earth moving.

NIC:	Yeah he was grasping for straws there…but he was trying, OK? He just didn't know about gravity and the power of the moon and that stuff yet. Hey you've got a heads up on old Galileo, don't you?
ELOISE:	I read some goofy kid's book once. So what happened to him?
NIC:	You read the book. Don't you remember?
ELOISE:	He wrote that kind of play thing.
NIC:	Right. *Dialogue on the Two Chief World Systems: Ptolemaic and Copernican.* He tried to disguise what he was saying by putting arguments into the mouths of three characters—you know, trying to make it seem like he was giving all points of view. Only problem was that the words of the Pope were made to sound stupid while the words of the Galileo character sounded exceedingly logical. So they ordered him to stand trial on suspicion of heresy and convicted him. Lucky for him he had lots of pals in high places so he wasn't burned alive. But under house arrest for the rest of his days.
ELOISE:	For being right. It's so stupid.
NIC:	That's what you get for saying things that folks don't want to hear.

Pause. NIC looks up.

You know Galileo was also the first guy to figure out that the Milky Way wasn't just a cloud but a multitude of stars. Look at them. And Jupiter as clear as day and it's millions and millions of miles away. We are looking at the same skies that Galileo looked at, give or take a satellite or two. It just boggles my mind. Living in the city you forget about the magnitude of it all, but here… I can't help it. I look up at those night skies and feel completely insignificant… I feel overwhelmed by

questions. Do those stars go on and on forever? Or
is there an end to it all. And if there is an end, what
is that? How can there be an end? Doesn't an end
to something signify something else beginning?
And then I think what a miracle it is we are here
at all. Or is it? Maybe it has to be from some
kind of divine design. The scientific side of me,
of course, says no. We are a just a whim of luck.
Life slowly materialized out of the Big Bang. But
then my spiritual side says how can that be? This
wondrous beauty must be part of a bigger plan. It's
all so miraculous. Trees are miraculous. Insects are
miraculous. Babies! And when I look up at those
stars I think is it naïve for us to think we are the
only intelligent creatures in the universe. Earth
cannot be the only place where life exists. Not with
the other solar systems that must be out there. And
going along that line of thinking then we probably
aren't the smartest lights in the sky either. I mean
look how we're tipping the balance of nature right
off its axis. It makes logical sense that there are
beings out there who are more advanced than us.
Who have mastered interplanetary travel. Who are
watching us. Observing us. Perhaps occasionally
interacting. The scientific community is very
divided about this. Most will smile knowingly and
say yes there probably is life on other planets. But
if you push them to commit to admitting to alien
life forms they get very evasive. That's our current
cultural climate. It's only supermarket tabloids
that talk about UFOs. It's just silly. It's not cool to
say you've seen a strange configuration of lights
hovering fifteen feet away from you? Is it, Eloise?

ELOISE: No. It isn't. But actually as it turns out I didn't see
              anything strange. It was somebody playing a cruel
              joke.

NIC: Is that so?

ELOISE: Somebody called and told me. Today. So that's what I was talking to Christine Clark about. She's going to write a new article for the *Clarion*. Set the record straight.

NIC: You'll be coming back to school then.

ELOISE: Yeah.

NIC: That's good. You know I was talking to Mr. Richards. I told him I was thinking of starting a science club. And he told me about the science club that you started.

ELOISE: I wouldn't recommend it.

NIC: Why not?

ELOISE: Didn't he tell you how everybody made fun of us?

NIC: Yeah. I can never figure out why kids do that stupid stuff. But you know what really blew me away? That you were his top grade nine science student.

ELOISE: I lost interest.

NIC: I must be some rotten teacher.

ELOISE: I lost interest last year.

NIC: When the science club folded?

ELOISE: Around then.

NIC: When your dad died?

ELOISE: Close to that time. It was mixed up in a lot of things.

            Pause.

NIC: You know, I was kinda hoping you had seen something. I love reading books about Roswell and other UFO stuff. My guilty pleasure.

ELOISE: Roswell?

NIC: In New Mexico. Where that farmer found all sorts of metal scattered over his field. In the forties. You heard about this, right?

ELOISE: No.

NIC: No? This metal was unlike anything ever been seen before. Couldn't be scratched, burned, ripped, cut… had strange geometric hieroglyphs. So the farmer gets a Major Marcel from a local airbase to come check it out and he couldn't believe his eyes. This metal stuff was scattered three quarters of a mile long and three hundred feet wide. Something huge crashed in that field. Something beyond Earthly knowledge. The local Air Force actually issues a press release stating they had evidence of a flying saucer. The local paper even prints up the story. But before you can say Extra-Terrestrial, Washington issues a shut-up edict. Gathers up every smidgeon of that debris and ships it off to some fort. Anyone even thinking about saying it's a UFO is told to cease and desist in no uncertain terms. The official story is that it was a weather balloon. Poor old Major Marcel was made to pose with some ripped up old balloon, he looks absolutely shell-shocked in the picture. The farmer supported the balloon story—though it seems he got a new truck and an inflated bank account out of the deal.

ELOISE: But you think he was lying? That it was a space ship?

NIC: I wouldn't say this at a local community meeting but, yes, I think the evidence is very strong in that direction. Although some folks think it was some advanced US army rocket ship. I don't buy it. But that's part of the fun. The debate. Of course I don't go along with the whole shebang. That they found four little grey men, one still alive, kept under lock and key eating strawberry ice cream. I don't go for all that. But some things just can't be explained away.

Pause.

Such as...my dog barking like crazy a week ago Friday night about half past midnight. And a young woman banging on my door; terrified out of her wits. And me feeling paralysed to do anything to help her.

Pause.

ELOISE: That was your house?

NIC: Yes.

ELOISE: Your dog?

NIC: Yes.

ELOISE: What kind of dog?

NIC: Black and white mutt. Answers to the name of Ebenezer.

ELOISE: You live on the Burns line?

NIC: Yes.

ELOISE: Why didn't you... Why are you telling me this. Now

NIC: Because I feel pretty guilty about not saying something earlier.

ELOISE: You can just leave. I don't want to talk to you.

          ELOISE snatches up the work he has brought and starts to go into the house.

NIC: I don't blame you for feeling upset, Eloise. I lied. I absolutely bald-faced lied. That woman came to my house and I denied ever having seen or heard anything.

ELOISE: You're a complete shithead. You know that? And I don't care if you are my teacher.

NIC: Right now, in this moment, I would have to agree with you.

ELOISE: Didn't you hear me calling for help?

NIC: I did, yes.

ELOISE: Did you know it was me?

NIC: Not at first but...

ELOISE: Why? What kind of person are you?

NIC: I have no excuse. You are perfectly right to be angry.

ELOISE: Angry? That doesn't even begin to cover what I feel. Just you wait. Just you— I'm going to spread it all over the school that you are one big fat shithead.

NIC: Eloise...I understand your frustration, but that isn't going to help.

ELOISE: You have completely ruined my life. Christine Clark would have believed you, a teacher. She would have believed me if there was one little sign that I was telling the truth.

NIC: I know that. And I'm sorry.

ELOISE: Sorry isn't good enough.

NIC: I was afraid.

ELOISE: Afraid of what?! What could you possibly be afraid of?

NIC: Eloise! Think for yourself! I'm a single Black man in a white town. Living alone. A pretty young student is found with me, in a ripped dress, screaming and crying for help.

Pause.

ELOISE: That's why you lied to her?

NIC: That's part of it. Yes.

ELOISE: Because you were afraid that people would suspect you of having something creepy with one of your students?

NIC: Yes.

ELOISE: What's the other part?

NIC: What do you mean?

ELOISE: You said that was part of it, what's the other part?

Pause.

Oh my gawd, you saw it, didn't you? You saw it too.

Pause.

What did you see?!

NIC: Oh, boy.

ELOISE: Tell me. You owe me.

NIC: I heard Ebenezer barking. Out of his mind. So I got out of bed thinking there must be an animal, a coyote or something.

ELOISE: Yeah?

NIC: But before I even got to the window I noticed the light. Bright, like sunlight, shining through the window. And I saw it, exactly how you described. Floating above the ground, moving, and shimmering in front of me. I couldn't move. Like I was hypnotized. And a moment later…it was over. I heard you calling and banging. I could see you on the porch and all I could see was trouble. For both of us. I watched you, sitting there… I figured you were safe.

ELOISE: OK. You want to set things right? You can go to Christine now, tonight, and tell her what you saw. She'd print it. I know she would.

NIC: That's not going to happen, Eloise.

ELOISE: Why not?

NIC: I haven't actually made a sterling impression in this town.

ELOISE: What are you talking about?

NIC: Back in August I went to a meeting about the possibility of bringing French Immersion in to the school. I thought it was good idea. My Dad grew up in Montreal and I absolutely believe kids should have a second language. Helps them get jobs. Or if they travel. So…at the meeting I was very vocal, speaking strongly in favour. The looks I got… That Mrs. Barber still can't look me in the eye. Wow. I learned pretty quick that things are done differently here. Tradition is really important to folks. And I have to respect that.

ELOISE: So? That makes what you did OK?

NIC: So. That makes me a coward. I guess.

ELOISE: And I guess you think me lying to Christine Clark is a good idea? Pretend the whole thing never happened.

NIC: I'm hardly one to make any judgments. Believe me I thought very carefully about putting you out of your misery but…I guess I'm not the man I wish I was.

ELOISE: I guess not.

NIC: There's more. You're really going to like this.
            The next day...I, the defender of free speech and
            science, actually went out there and destroyed the
            evidence. The grass had been completely flattened,
            there was even a odd mark pressed into the ground
            and I went over it with my lawnmower, my shovel,
            my rake to make absolutely sure there was no sign
            of anything.

ELOISE: You're a teacher, you're supposed to know better.

NIC: Well.

ELOISE: OK. I get this. There's some kind of Galileo
            connection here. I'm supposed to feel OK because
            I'm under house arrest for saying the truth and
            where does that leave you...you're the guy who
            looks away while they light the flames under the
            poor monk.

NIC: Eloise, please.

            Pause.

            I am very, very sorry.

ELOISE: Why did you come to this stupid old town in the
            first place ?

NIC: This? Are you joking? It's beautiful! The corn.
            The sunsets. The rolling hills. And the stars. My
            goodness. Look at those stars. Do you think I get
            all this in Toronto? I can hardly breathe there. Every
            smog alert day I ended up in Emerg with an asthma
            attack. And here, I've got a job doing what I love:
            boring students about the wonders of science.

ELOISE: You're not boring, you're just...

NIC: Weird?

ELOISE: A little.

NIC: Yeah. And there are good people here. You know, I came here with that big city attitude, feeling like I know it all but... You know that guy that runs the hardware store?

ELOISE: Mr. Gibbs?

NIC: He's made the most fantastic telescope from a kit he ordered off the internet. He knows way more than I do about these night skies. He's taught me tons of stuff.

ELOISE: Really?

NIC: I know some folks look at me like I'm some kind of alien... *(He smiles at this thought.)* ...but...others have been very kind.

Pause.

ELOISE: I thought I was going crazy. I was beginning to think I had imagined the whole thing.

NIC: I know. But...I am pretty sure you aren't going crazy. And if you are I am right behind you. I don't think you can manufacture what we saw. And... you know...now this is weird...I don't know if you felt this but...whatever it was...knew everything about me. About my fears and insecurities and cowardice. What ever it was was looking straight into my soul.

ELOISE: It was really something wasn't it? I haven't a clue whether it was something from another planet or whatever but it was...amazing. That light.

NIC: You know what it reminded me of? The Northern Lights. Not all the colours but...the dancing, rippling effect.

ELOISE: I know. And…you said it was like they could see inside you… They looked inside me too. It was like they could see my dad and how sad I was and everything. I didn't think they or it wanted to hurt me. They just wanted to look. They were sad for me. Didn't you feel that? That they know us so well. They know how pathetic we all are. Didn't you feel that?

NIC: Something like that.

ELOISE: And then it just disappeared out there, with the stars. Like it never happened.

NIC: Yeah.

           Pause.

ELOISE: You know there's a line of Shakespeare that when my dad was dying kept going through my head. I used to read Shakespeare to him at the hospital sometimes, I never knew if he was wincing from the pain or my reading but… Something like… "and when he shall die, take him, and cut him out in little stars and he shall make the face of heaven so fine that all the world will be in love with night, and pay no worship to the garish sun."

NIC: *Romeo and Juliet.*

ELOISE: So sometimes. When I look at the stars I think they are him. All cut out and up there twinkling. Pretty stupid huh?

NIC: No it isn't stupid. That is a lovely thought, Miss Eloise Bernhardt. A big whopper of a lovely thought.

           They both look up at the stars.

Scene 6

GLENN is bustling around the kitchen, making a special breakfast. She pours ELOISE some orange juice. After a moment ELOISE comes down the stairs, dressed for school.

GLENN: You're up early. I wasn't going to wake you for a half an hour.

ELOISE: What's all this?

GLENN: Birthday breakfast. French toast. Wild blueberries and peaches and real maple syrup.

ELOISE: Sounds yummy.

GLENN: I'll have three slices on a plate before you know it... Happy Birthday Sweet 16.

ELOISE: Thanks.

GLENN: Now sit down. We haven't really decided what we're going to do for your birthday. Do you want to have some friends over?

ELOISE: No.

GLENN: Did you call Aunty Bobbie?

ELOISE: No but I will. I promise. After school.

GLENN: You're going to school today?

ELOISE: Yup.

GLENN: Good. Did that Mr. Barlow catch you up on all the science work?

ELOISE: Yup.

GLENN: He stayed for quite a while. What were you talking about?

ELOISE: He wanted to know about that science club we had last year and that kind of stuff.

GLENN: And did you tell him?

ELOISE: Some.

GLENN: He looks nice.

ELOISE: He's OK.

GLENN: You know I was thinking about...maybe you want to talk to Liz and make sure we get our stories straight. Liz could say that she heard someone played some kind of joke. She won't say who. Maybe the two of you can think of some detail... like...tire tracks or something that made you think it was a prank.

ELOISE: I've already talked to Christine. I called her last night and told her not to write anything more.

GLENN: You did? Why didn't you talk to me before—

ELOISE: You told me I was the only one who would know what the right thing to do is and that is what I think is right. I just want to leave it alone.

GLENN: Are you sure?

ELOISE: Everyone will want to know who did it and...it will never end. This way...I just won't say anything and they can think what they want.

GLENN: I thought you said Larry Delray might have done something—

ELOISE: Larry Delray is living in Owen Sound now. I don't think he was within fifty kilometers of me that night.

GLENN: What about—

ELOISE: Mum. Leave it.

GLENN: OK. Alright. Good. That's very grown up of you... But...I...just don't want people thinking that you thought—

ELOISE: I can't care my whole life what people think, can I? Or I'll never go out. I'll never do anything. I'll never do well in science again if I care so much what everybody thinks. Is that what you want?

GLENN: No. I don't.

GLENN puts the French toast down in front of ELOISE.

Sixteen. Holy smokes. It goes by so fast.

GLENN opens a drawer and takes out a birthday package. And places it front of ELOISE.

Before you get your hands all sticky. You had better open that.

ELOISE: Thank you

GLENN: It's not from me.

Pause.

When your father got to a point where he knew he wasn't going to get better...the thing that upset him the most is that he wouldn't be here to see you grow up. He thought about missing your sixteenth birthday and...when he was still well enough... He went out and bought that and wrapped it up and asked me to save it for you.

ELOISE: It's from Daddy?

GLENN: From your dear father, who loved you so much.

        ELOISE slowly takes the paper off. It's a lovely leather bound book.

ELOISE: *Romeo and Juliet.*

        She opens it up and reads the inscription. She smiles and perhaps cries a little. Then she goes to her mother and hugs her. They hold each other for a minute. ELOISE sits at her breakfast and drinks the orange juice.

You know what? I think I would like to see some of that Shakespeare shit with Aunty Bobbie. We can twang Smarties at the stage together.

        GLENN laughs a little then without ELOISE seeing she looks up and:

GLENN: *(Mouths silently.)* Thank you.

        The End.